Venus

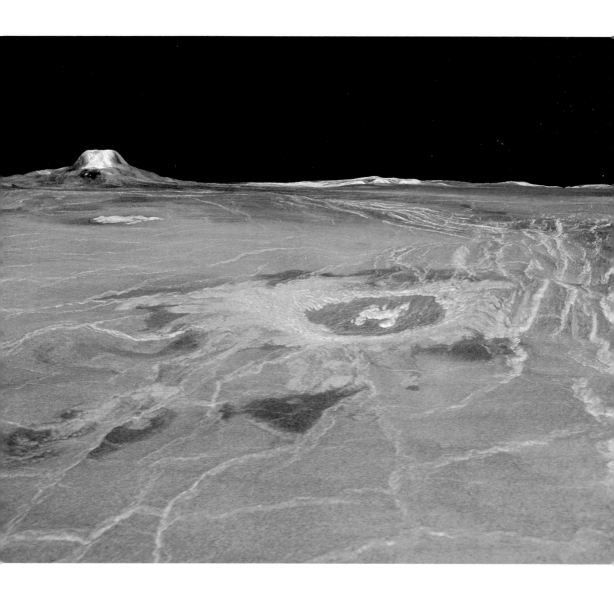

Other Voyage into Space Books

Star Guide

Uranus: *The Seventh Planet*

Superstar: *The Supernova of 1987*

Neptune: *Voyager's Final Target*

A Voyage into Space Book

Venus

Magellan Explores Our Twin Planet
by Franklyn M. Branley

HarperCollins*Publishers*

Photos courtesy of NASA/JPL
Painting, page 12, courtesy of Helmut K. Wimmer
Illustrations, pages 7, 8, 10, & 42 by David Cain

ACKNOWLEDGMENTS

I want to thank so many for their help and suggestions,
especially Tim Bridges of McDonnell Douglas,
Carolynn Young of the Jet Propulsion Laboratory, and
Kathleen Zoehfeld, my editor, who put it all together.

Library of Congress Cataloging-in-Publication Data
Branley, Franklyn Mansfield, date
    Venus : Magellan explores our twin planet / by Franklyn M. Branley.
        p.   cm. — (A Voyage into space book)
    Includes bibliographical references and index.
    Summary: Describes the topography and motions of the planet Venus, explains theories
about its origin and evolution, and presents recent discoveries made by the Magellan
spacecraft.
    ISBN 0-06-020298-X. — ISBN 0-06-020384-6 (lib. bdg.)
    1. Venus (Planet)—Exploration—Juvenile literature.   2. Magellan (Spacecraft)—Juvenile
literature. [1. Venus (Planet)   2. Magellan (Spacecraft)]   I. Title.   II. Series.
QB621.B7 1994   92-32990
523.4'2—dc20   CIP
                                                                          AC

Typography by Al Cetta
1   2   3   4   5   6   7   8   9   10
❖
First Edition

Contents

Venus

1. Magellan Reaches Venus

On May 4, 1989, the space shuttle Atlantis lifted off from NASA's Kennedy Space Center in Florida. Stowed carefully in the cargo bay was Magellan, the first planet probe to be carried aloft by a shuttle.

Shortly after going into orbit around Earth, the crew of Atlantis launched Magellan from the cargo bay. The probe was set free. Its booster rocket was fired, and the journey to Venus had begun. After fifteen months, Magellan eased into orbit around our sister planet. The probe began to survey Venus in more detail than had ever been done before.

Magellan's instrument for observing the surface of Venus is a radar. It measures the altitude of Venusian features such as mountains, plateaus, cliffs, and valleys and takes "pictures" of the surface. Cameras cannot be used to get these pictures, because the planet is covered with dense clouds. It is impossible to see through them. But radar can help us "see" through them in a different way.

The orbit of Magellan is elliptical. Therefore its distance from the planet varies. When it is at the farthest point in its orbit, it is 5,224 miles away from the planet; when closest it is only 158 miles away. During the close approach, which lasts for 20 minutes, Magellan's radar instrument bounces radio waves off the planet's surface. After the waves strike the surface, they reflect back to the probe, where they are recorded.

As Magellan reaches the far point of its orbit, the probe turns its antenna and sends its recorded information to Earth, where computers turn the data into pictures. About three hours later Magellan is again close to the planet, and another survey is made.

Magellan flies from north to south, almost over the poles of Venus. The planet turns beneath the probe's orbit. During the time it is close to the planet, Magellan's radar scans a strip of Venus that is 15 miles wide and 9,300 miles long. After eight months most of the planet had been scanned. Then Magellan repeated the operation. If

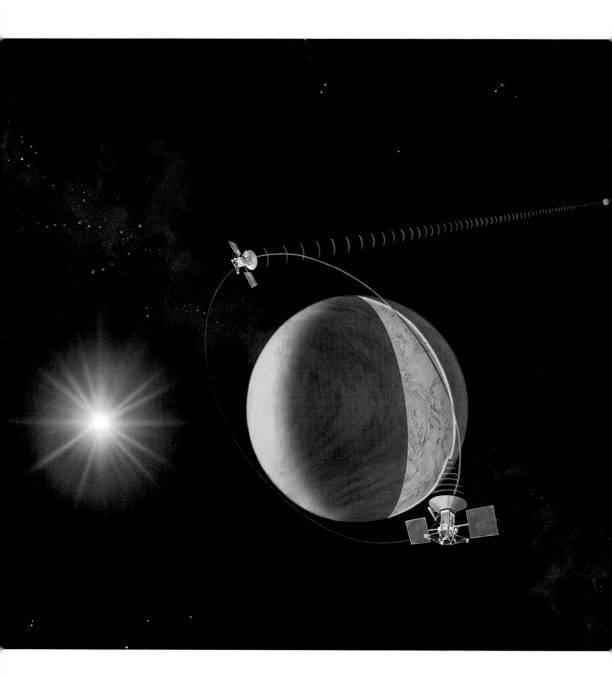

changes are occurring on the surface, such as volcanic eruptions, they may be revealed by comparing one scan to another. So far, no such changes have been seen.

Magellan is not the first probe to visit Venus. It is the latest in a long series of probes that have been launched by the United States and by the former Soviet Union. In fact, more probes have been sent to Venus than to any other planet. It is our nearest neighbor. But it is a mysterious neighbor. Scientists have long been curious to discover what lies under its thick clouds.

Soviet Venera probes, and the more recent Vega probes, have landed on the surface of the planet and released balloons that have collected information about the atmosphere. The Pioneer Venus spacecraft sent by the United States in 1978 made radar maps of the surface. Later, Venera probes also made radar maps. They were very good, but not nearly as clear and detailed as the scans made by Magellan.

Before space probes began to be sent in the 1960s, the only information we had about Venus was obtained by using Earth-based telescopes.

2. The Motions of Venus: Phases, Days, and Years

Phases

The first person to see Venus through a telescope was the Italian astronomer Galileo Galilei. In 1609 he made the first telescope used in astronomy. The telescope was not very powerful, yet Galileo made many discoveries with it. One thing he found was that Venus goes through a cycle of changes, or phases, just as the Moon does. Without a telescope these changes cannot be seen. Galileo explained that Venus goes through phases because it moves in an or-

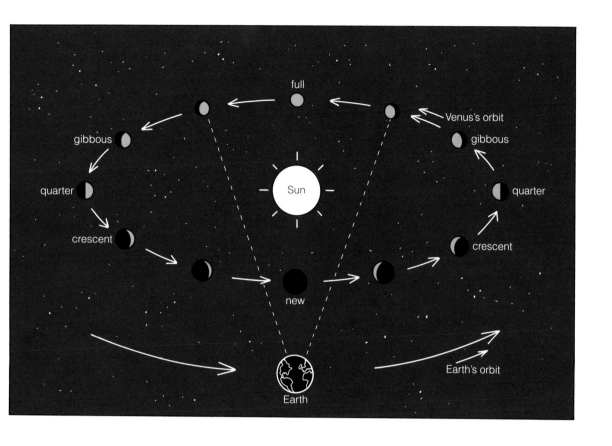

bit that is closer to the Sun than Earth's orbit. And he was right!

Sometimes during its orbit Venus is between us and the Sun. At such times the dark side of the planet is toward us, and we cannot see it. This is called the new phase. A few days later Venus has moved along its orbit. Through a telescope we see a long, thin crescent. A few days later, the crescent has grown fatter, and it is much brighter.

After several weeks Venus will appear as a quarter planet. It will continue toward becoming full. At that time we will be on one side of the Sun and Venus will be on the other. When Venus is full, it is in the solar glare, and we cannot see it. After the full phase the cycle of events is repeated in reverse order. In its crescent phases the planet is some 26 million miles from us. It is about 160 million miles away when it is full. A complete cycle of changes, from the new phase back to the new phase again, takes 512 days.

As seen through a telescope, the apparent size of Venus grows as it moves from its full to its crescent and new phases. When full, it is farthest from us and so smallest and dim. When crescent, it is much closer to us and therefore bright. In its new phase Venus is nearest to us and so largest, but we cannot see it—the dark half is toward us.

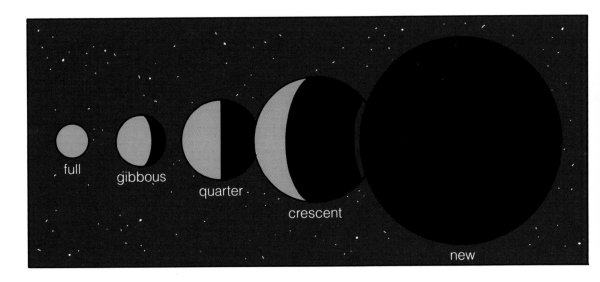

full gibbous quarter crescent new

Since Mercury also orbits between the Sun and the Earth's orbit, it shows phases too. The outer planets do not, because their orbits are outside our own.

The orbit of Venus is between Earth's and the Sun, and so we can see the planet only by looking in the general direction of the Sun. We cannot see Venus at midnight, when we are facing directly away from the Sun. We see Venus only at twilight, a few hours after the Sun has set or a few hours before the Sun rises. We see the planet as an "evening star" or a "morning star."

In early days people believed Venus was a star—in fact, they believed it was two different stars; one that they saw in the evening and one that appeared in the morning, just before sunrise. The evening star was called Hesperus; the morning star was Phosphorus. The name Hesperus comes from a Greek word meaning western, while Phosphorus is from Greek words meaning "the bringer of light."

Days and Years

The closer an object is to the Sun, the faster it must move to keep from being pulled into it. Mercury, the closest planet, moves 29.69 miles a second. Pluto, which in 1999 and for some 200 years thereafter will be the farthest planet, moves only 2.94 miles in one second. Venus is

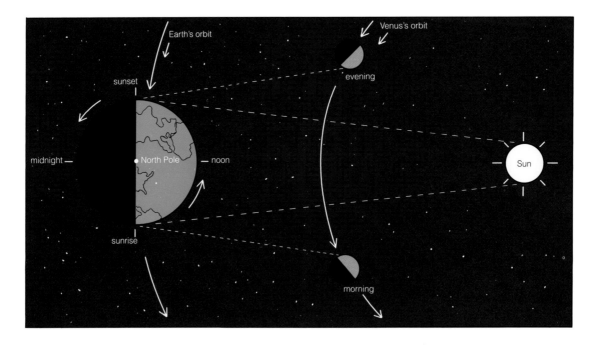

When Venus is in position 1, we see it as a morning object (Phosphorus), just before we see the Sun. When Venus is in position 2, it is an evening object (Hesperus): The Sun sets below the horizon, the sky darkens, and Venus becomes visible. After a short time, it also sets. (Sizes and distances are not to scale.)

closer to the Sun than we are. Earth is 92.75 million miles away, while Venus is 64.92 million miles from our central star. Therefore Venus must travel faster than we do. It goes 21.72 miles a second, and Earth goes 18.54 miles a second. Because Venus travels faster than we do, and because its orbit is shorter than ours, it completes an orbit in less time than we do. A year on Venus is 224.73 Earth days long; a year on Earth is 365.25 days.

While Venus goes around the Sun, it also rotates, as do all the planets. We rotate from west to east. On Earth, therefore, the Sun rises in the east and sets in the west. Venus rotates backward—from east to west. Sunrise on Venus is in the west, and sunset is in the east. Also, the planet rotates more slowly than any other planet. It takes 243 days to make a complete turn.

Venus has two sunrises and two sunsets during the course of one rotation. On Venus a given location has sunrise every 117 Earth days. If you were on Venus and could see the Sun (both highly unlikely), you would see it rise in the west, and 58.5 days later it would be setting in the east. Sunrise and sunset on Venus would both last a long time. It takes almost a month for the Sun to reach the overhead, or noontime, location and another month to move from noon to sunset.

Sunrise and sunset on Venus are quite different from what we experience on Earth. Perhaps you have noticed that as the Sun gets closer to the horizon, it gets redder and loses its roundness. It is flattened, looking something like a beach ball when you sit on it. This happens because when we look toward the Sun on the horizon, we see it through many layers of atmosphere. Sunlight coming to us

through these layers is bent, much as light is bent by a lens. This bending distorts the shape of the Sun. Also, the layers of atmosphere allow red light to come through to us and scatter the other colors that make up sunlight.

On Venus the atmosphere is much denser than it is on Earth. Therefore, the bending of sunlight is greater. It is so great that at sunrise and sunset the image of the Sun is almost completely flattened along the horizon. It is thickest at the Sun itself and thins as the distance from the Sun increases.

Sunset on Venus might look something like this. (The image of the Sun is shown in a few locations in order to show its changing appearance as it sets.)

3. The Evolution of Venus

Venus's slow rotation and dense atmosphere are unusual among the planets. But like the other planets, Venus formed some 4.6 billion years ago out of dust and gases contained in the great gaseous cloud out of which the entire solar system was born. About half a billion years earlier, the Sun had formed, using most of the material in the cloud. Venus and the other planets were made of "leftover" material.

The cloud was layered, with a large percentage of the denser substances, such as iron and nickel, closer to the

Sun. As distance from the Sun increased, the density of the material decreased. In the outer part of the cloud, there was mostly hydrogen. The inner planets, Mercury, Venus, Earth, and Mars, were formed from the inner, denser part of the cloud. It seems likely that the four planets were originally made of the same relative percentages of hydrogen, carbon, oxygen, iron, nickel, and so on. Down through billions of years, though, tremendous changes have occurred on all the planets. Although Venus and Earth are sometimes called the twin planets, they have become quite different in many ways.

The planets are called twins because they are almost the same size. The diameter of Earth is 7,927 miles; the diameter of Venus is 7,503 miles. The mass of the two planets (the amount of material they contain) is also about the same. If the mass of Earth is 1, the mass of Venus is 0.82—just a bit lower. And the density of the material in the two planets is almost the same. If you could weigh the whole Earth, you would find that it weighs 5.52 times the weight of an equal volume of water. The density of Earth, then, is 5.52. The density of Venus is 5.25, nearly the same. Although the two planets arose in the same way, and although they have many similarities, scientists are challenged to explain the events that caused the differences we see in the planets today.

Here on Earth our atmosphere is mostly nitrogen (80

Earth is a lush planet with lakes, rivers, and oceans. White clouds of water vapor float in the atmosphere.

percent) and oxygen (about 20 percent), with small amounts of argon, carbon dioxide, neon, helium, hydrogen, and other gases.

The atmosphere of Venus is very different. It contains small amounts of nitrogen, water, sulfur, and neon. There

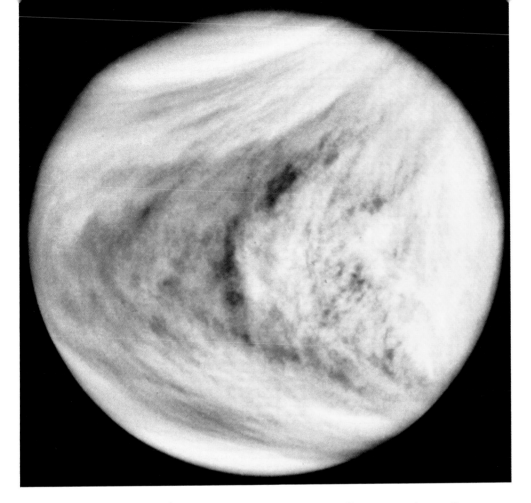

Droplets of sulfuric acid, dry-ice particles (frozen carbon dioxide), and dust make up dense clouds that cover Venus.

is a considerable amount of sulfur dioxide, which when it combines with the water becomes sulfuric acid droplets—acid rain. But fully 90 percent of the atmosphere is carbon dioxide.

Because of its nearness to the Sun, Venus has become

very hot, so hot that its oceans have boiled away. On Earth our oceans absorb carbon dioxide from the atmosphere. On Venus the carbon dioxide remains in the atmosphere.

Scientists reason that at one time the two planets had similar amounts of water. But there is little water on Venus

Under the clouds, Venus is a dry and barren place. This global map of Venus's surface was put together using radar images from Magellan.

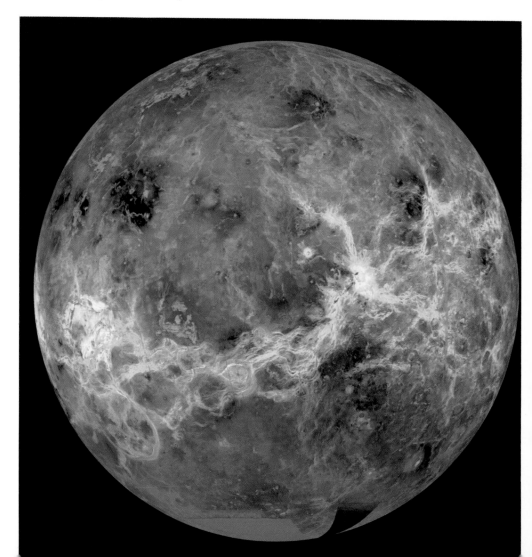

now and certainly no oceans, lakes, or rivers. Where did the water go?

Possibly, early in the planet's history, the Sun heated Venus to high temperatures. Steam rose from the oceans, and the atmosphere of the planet became laden with hot water vapor. Sunlight would have broken apart the water molecules in the atmosphere, changing them to free oxygen and hydrogen. The hydrogen would then have escaped from the atmosphere—lost in space. Some of the oxygen in the air, together with some of the carbon, would have been absorbed by rocks. But large amounts of carbon would have combined with oxygen and remained in the atmosphere as carbon dioxide.

After a few hundred million years, most of the water of the planet had disappeared. Presently, a little water vapor remains in the atmosphere, though it is one thousandth of the amount in ours. There is a thousand times more carbon dioxide in Venus's atmosphere than in ours.

Since Venus has no lakes, rivers, streams, or rainfall, there has been little erosion on the planet. Water is the main cause of erosion here on Earth—wearing down the high places and filling in the low areas.

An important process in creating the present-day surface of Venus has been (and may continue to be) the action of volcanoes. In the early days of its history (billions of years ago) Venus was struck by storms of rocky meteorites, which created thousands of impact craters. How-

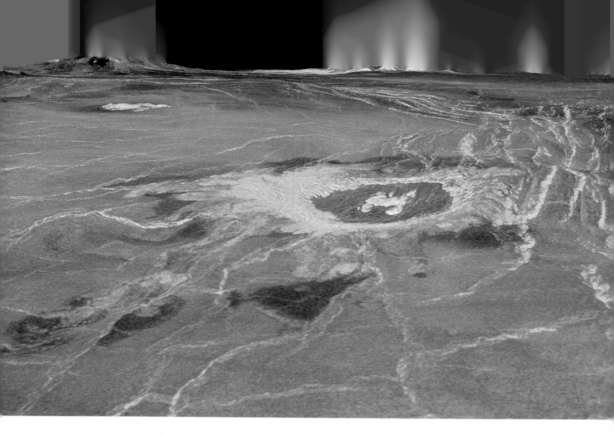

If you could get aboard a space probe and fly in for a bird's-eye view of the planet's surface, you might see a sight such as this one. This is a computer-enhanced picture based on some of Magellan's radar images.

ever, craters of this type are not abundant on the planet today. Only about 900 craters have been identified in Magellan images. Relatively recent volcanic activity (within the last several million years) has erased most traces of the earlier cratering.

A volcanic rock called basalt appears to be common on the surface. Also, Magellan's images show rounded domes that have probably been pushed up by underlying hot, molten rock, or magma. Or the domes may be pileups of thick lava that has oozed out to the surface. Elsewhere great rivers of hardened lava have been seen. Some extend for hundreds of miles yet may be only a mile or so across.

A major interest of scientists who study the Magellan scans is to see if volcanic eruptions or other changes are still occurring on the surface of our sister planet.

The fractured rocks in this photograph, taken by the space probe Venera 13, are probably basalt. Basalt is formed from hardened lava. (The toothed ring and leg are parts of the Venera lander.)

This is a Magellan radar image showing seven volcanic domes grouped in one area. The domes average about 15 miles across. They appear to be places where underlying magma once pushed up to the surface. The magma then receded a little, and the domes collapsed, creating the fractured surfaces we see on the domes today. (Magellan's radar images appear bright wherever the surface is rough.)

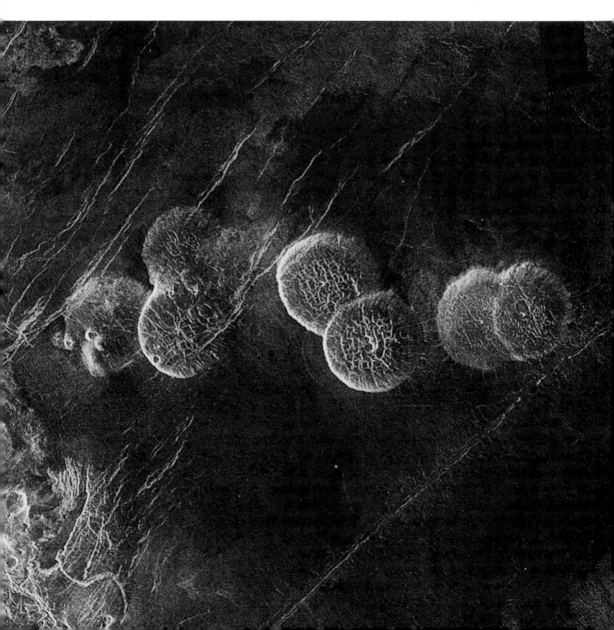

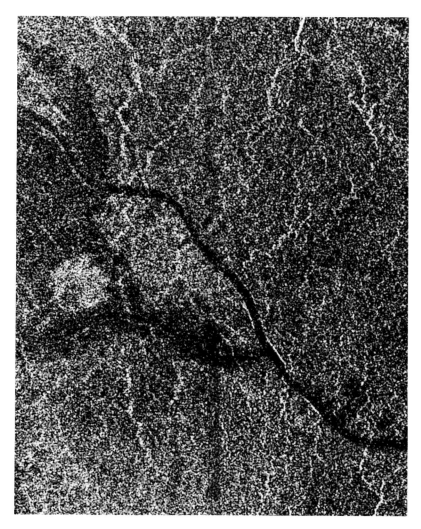

The dark ribbon in this radar image is a smooth lava flow, 1 mile wide and about 19 miles long, which appears to have formed from very fluid lava. (Magellan's images appear dark wherever the surface is smooth.) At the center, the lava spread out from the main channel. Today the lava flow is solid.

4. The Surface and Structure of Venus

Both Venus and Earth have mountains and valleys, plateaus and plains; however, the percentages of the different features vary. About 70 percent of Earth's surface is made of basins, extensive low areas that for the most part have become lakes and oceans. On Venus only 20 percent of the surface is basins. Some 20 percent of Earth's surface reaches above 6 miles (measuring from the lowest ocean basins to the tops of the highest mountains). On Venus only 11 percent of the surface is in that range.

No one understands completely how Earth's features

were formed. But it seems that a good many of them resulted from the action of plate tectonics.

Earth's crust is separated into huge sections called plates, most of which are larger than continents. These plates of solid material—some 60 miles thick in many places—float atop a layer called the mantle. The mantle is made of semimolten magma. The plates move very slowly, about as fast as your fingernails grow. In some areas they move apart, making tremendous rifts and valleys. One such formation extends north–south along the floor of the Atlantic Ocean. In other areas one plate may move under another, pushing rock layers upward and creating mountains. Lava may erupt through deep cracks that are made in the crust as the plates move. It is believed that most of the major features of our planet result from the motions of plates.

Venus also has mountains and deep rifts. And as we know, much of its surface shows evidence of volcanic activity. But plates do not seem to be moving on Venus. And they may never have been as large or extensive as they are on Earth. The problem, then, is to figure out what events or forces produced the formations on Venus.

Venus appears to have a thin crust. One theory says that the underlying layer of magma flowed slowly, grabbed onto the underside of the thin crust, and dragged it along. In some places the crust piled up into ridges, plateaus, and mountains. As the crust was dragged along, it stretched and became very thin in places. It split open and formed canyons and depressions. Some depressions may have extended into the layer of magma, allowing magma to well upward, making volcanic cones and mounds. As scientists study the sharper, more detailed images made by Magellan, other theories may develop.

Magellan made it possible to see features as small as 400 feet across. This is ten times better than the pictures made by the Soviet Veneras and by the U.S. Pioneer Venus.

The picture of the large impact crater Golubkina shows how much clearer the results from Magellan are than those obtained by the Veneras. Before Magellan we knew there was a crater, but as you can see, fine details of it were not revealed.

Clearly there is a central peak, and the rim is made of several terraces. The outside of the rim is bright. Reflected radar signals appear bright whenever the surface is uneven. The floor of the crater is black, which is the radar result when the surface is smooth.

Golubkina is about 20 miles across. There appear to be no impact craters on Venus that are less than about 5 miles across. This means all the meteorites that have hit the planet within the last few million years have been above a certain size. Any smaller meteorites would have been bro-

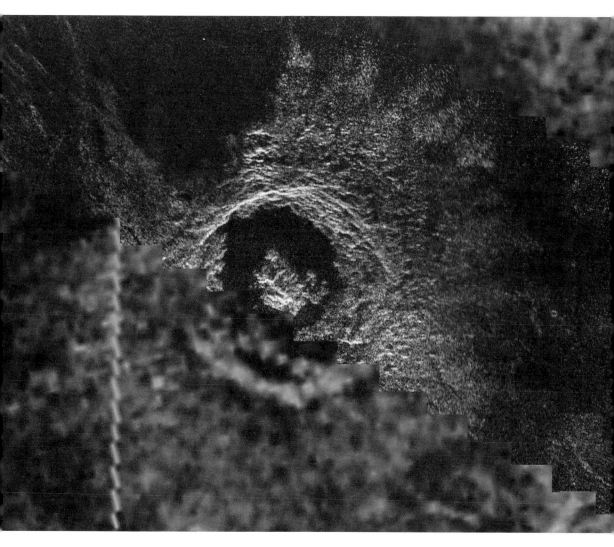

The left-hand side of this picture is a radar image made by a Venera space probe in the mid 1980s, showing half of the crater Golubkina. The right-hand side of the picture shows the other half of Golubkina, surveyed by Magellan's radar.

ken up and incinerated as they sped through the dense atmosphere of the planet.

Here are more of Magellan's pictures:

A group of interconnected fractures in a region of Venus's southern hemisphere. The fractures range from only a few hundred feet up to a few miles wide. The lines of small pits that appear here and there may be small volcanoes that formed as the crust fractured. Possibly the crust was pulled apart, or sections of it may have sunk.

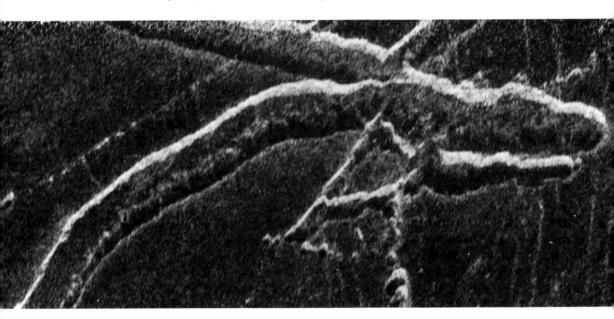

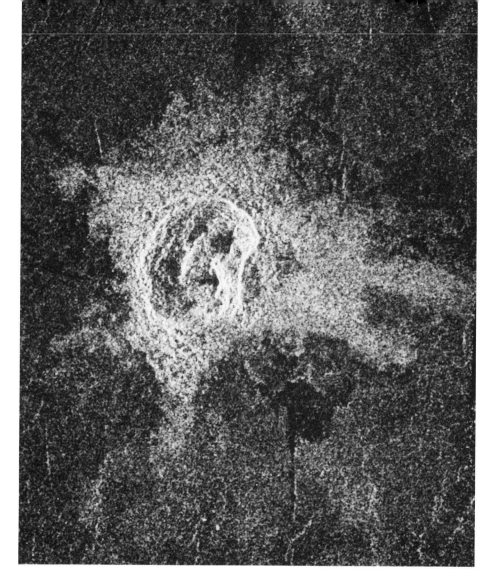

This kidney-shaped crater may have been formed by a meteorite that crashed into the planet. The meteorite may have broken up just before impact. The chunks fell side by side, creating the crater's unique shape. Dark patches may be lava that was ejected by a series of small volcanoes that could have been triggered by the impact.

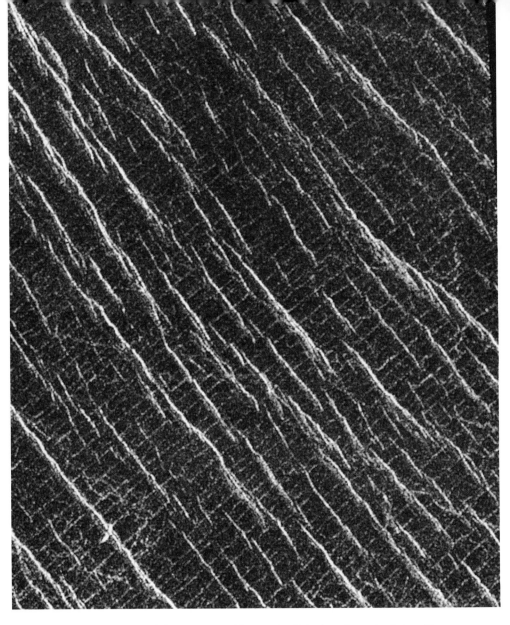

A most unusual feature on Venus is this fractured plain. Running one way are fine, straight, bright lines, showing rifts and valleys. At right angles to the valleys are more extensive high formations.

At the middle is an explosive volcano. The bright material is ash blown to the surface and drifted by wind. The cross-hatched fracturing of the surface around the volcano may have been caused by the rapid cooling and "wrinkling" of the surface.

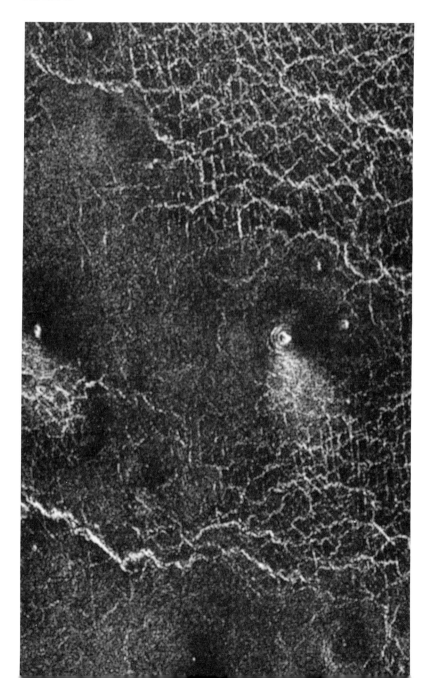

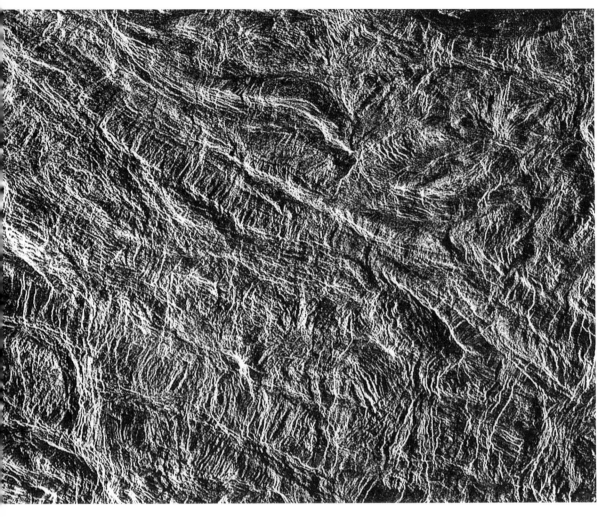

This area, about 78 miles long and 93 miles wide, shows the effects of folding, faulting, shearing, and stretching on the planet's surface. It seems the region has undergone many events of horizontal motion—perhaps these surface layers were pulled along by movements of underlying magma.

A computer-enhanced view of a group of craters called the "crater farm." The three craters were made when large meteorites crashed into the planet, pulverizing rock. The rock particles were thrown into the air and spread around the craters. The smallest crater shown here is about 25 miles across; the largest is about 45 miles.

Notice that the floors of the craters are smooth, and that each has a central peak. At impact, the surface of the planet is pushed down. As it springs back, material is ejected, forming the central peaks.

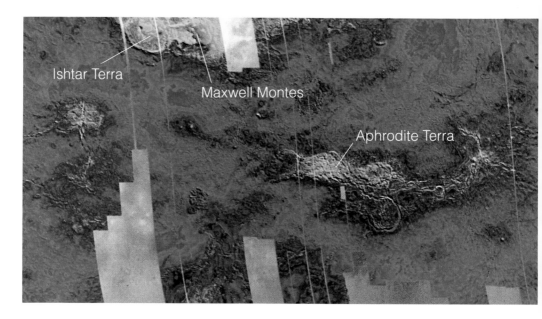

Ishtar Terra

Maxwell Montes

Aphrodite Terra

Magellan's map of Venus. This version is color-coded to make it easier to "read." Lowlands are blue. Mountainous areas are yellow and red. The gray strips are areas that have not been scanned.

Data from Magellan were put together to make the map shown on this page. The map shows there are two main highland features. They are called Ishtar Terra and Aphrodite Terra, after ancient goddesses. (By international agreement the features of Venus, with only a few exceptions, are named after women.)

The Ishtar Terra region stands several miles above the average planetary radius, which is the basis for measuring altitude on Venus. On Earth, altitude is measured from sea level. Of course, sea level cannot be used as a base level on Venus since there are no seas. The Ishtar region is larger than the entire United States. Its central part, Lakshmi Plateau, is a tableland, some 1,200 miles across, that is ringed by chains of volcanic mountains. The plateau may be an extensive lava flow from these volcanoes.

A computer-enhanced view of Maat Mons, a volcano some five miles high, in the Aphrodite Terra region. Maat Mons may be an active volcano. Scientists will watch it carefully to see if any changes occur.

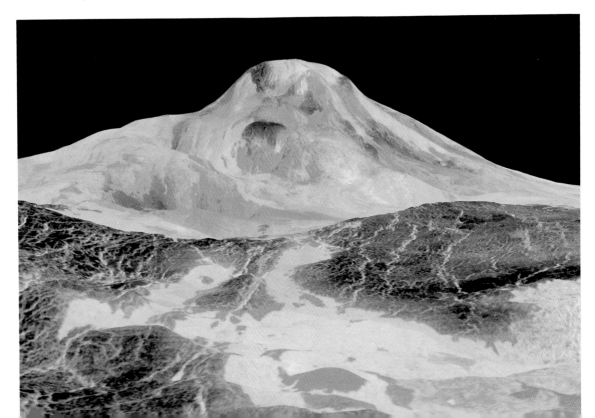

Maxwell Montes, in the Ishtar region, is the highest mountain on Venus. It is named after James Clerk Maxwell, an English scientist who made many discoveries in magnetism and electricity. Some of his work in mathematics made possible the early radar observations of Venus.

Aphrodite Terra is a very extensive region of highlands. It is about half the size of Africa. Canyons 2 miles deep, hundreds of miles wide, and 600 miles long cut through the region.

5. Magnetism

Many of the surface features of Venus and Earth are similar. Others are quite different. The same could be said about the interior features of the two planets. Earth is magnetic. It behaves as though it had a huge magnet inside it, one that extends from the north magnetic pole to the south magnetic pole. You can see an effect of Earth's magnetism with a compass. The needle takes a north-south direction, no matter where you happen to be.

This would also be true on Mercury, Jupiter, Saturn, Uranus, and Neptune. But not on Venus or Mars, or, we believe, on Pluto. (Probes have not visited Pluto, so measurements have not been made. However, it is thought that if magnetism does exist there, it is extremely weak.)

Earth's magnetism is thought to be a result of the presence of a liquid outer core and its movement against a semimolten mantle. The outer core lies below the mantle. Beneath the outer core is a solid central core of iron and nickel. The great pressure at the center of the Earth keeps the metal solid in spite of the high temperature. The outer core, on the other hand, is almost as fluid as water. It flows up and down rapidly, a million times faster than the semimolten magma of the mantle moves. This moves so slowly, any changes that occur there take tens of millions of years. Changes in the outer core probably occur in only ten years or so. The rapid motion of the currents in the outer core, coupled with their movement against the mantle, produces an electric current, which creates Earth's magnetic field.

When a probe detects a magnetic field on another planet, it is assumed there is a liquid, or molten, metallic core, and probably a semimolten layer. Features observed on Venus's surface lead scientists to believe that the planet has a semimolten layer, though it is probably not as pliable as that of Earth. And it is believed by some scientists that Venus has a liquid core. Why then does Venus have little or no magnetism?

The planet's rotation (one turn in 243 days) may be too slow to produce strong currents in the planet's liquid core, which may also be much smaller and cooler than Earth's core. As a result, the liquid core may not flow enough to generate electricity.

The interior layers of Venus probably cooled more rapidly than Earth's did because Venus was hotter than our planet. That may not seem to make sense, but it does. Earth's thick crust slows the loss of heat from the interior. On Venus the crust is thin, so the very hot interior layers may have reached closer to the planet's unusually hot surface. The liquid material may have flowed easily to the surface. We see signs this may be true—the volcanic cones and lava flows that seem to be everywhere on the planet. The interior heat of Venus could get to the surface more readily than could the interior heat of Earth. Venus, which was hotter than Earth, cooled more rapidly than we did.

6. Temperature and Weather

Temperature

Even though Venus's interior layers are probably cooler than Earth's, Venus's climate remains the hottest of all the planets. Earth is warm along the equator, and it is cold in the polar regions. In areas between the equator and the poles, temperatures change as the seasons go by, and as daytime alternates with night. Although there are changes in local temperatures, and there are places that are always hot or cold, the temperature of the entire Earth—averaging all regions together—is close to 60° Fahrenheit.

Not so on Venus. Year in and year out, during both day and night, and in all locations the temperature holds close to 860°F. That is twice as hot as a hot oven. Certainly the heat is enough to make it impossible for any life as we know it to survive. From Earth we see Venus as a bright, pleasant-appearing planet, but it is far from being serene and comfortable.

Since Venus is a lot closer to the Sun than we are, it receives a lot more energy from the Sun than we do. That partly explains why the planet is hotter than we are. But a phenomenon known as the greenhouse effect is another important factor causing the high temperature of Venus.

Much of the heat in a greenhouse is trapped solar energy. Sunlight, which is shortwave radiation, passes through the glass or plastic cover of a greenhouse. When this radiation strikes the soil and plants in a greenhouse, it changes to infrared (heat) radiation. Infrared is long-wave radiation. These long waves cannot readily escape through the cover of the greenhouse. The heat is trapped, and so the temperature inside the greenhouse rises.

That is what happens on Venus. The carbon dioxide that makes up most of Venus's atmosphere covers the planet like a blanket; it acts like a greenhouse cover. Strong, shortwave sunlight shines through the carbon dioxide. When the sunlight reaches the surface of the planet, it changes to long-wave infrared heat. These long

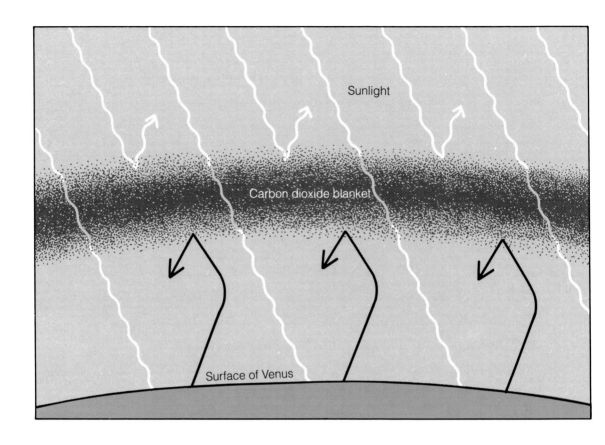

waves cannot pass easily through the carbon dioxide, so they are trapped. Temperature goes up to a high level, and it stays there.

As we know, most of Earth's carbon dioxide has been dissolved in seawater. The amount of carbon dioxide remaining in Earth's atmosphere is not enough to act as a greenhouse cover. Therefore, Earth does not heat up the way Venus does. We warm up during the day, but heat escapes after the Sun has set.

Presently the amount of carbon dioxide in Earth's atmosphere is increasing slowly, and it has been doing so for the past century. People of today burn a lot of coal and oil. When these fuels are burned, carbon dioxide is produced. It may be more than the oceans can absorb. Some scientists believe that in about 50 years there will be so much carbon dioxide in the air that it will greatly increase the greenhouse effect. Heat would be captured, raising Earth's temperature four or five degrees Fahrenheit. That would be enough to cause partial melting of huge ice deposits in Greenland and Antarctica—enough to raise the surface of the oceans, which in turn would flood coastal cities. Weather patterns could change. Rain might fall in deserts. Areas that now enjoy plentiful rainfall might dry out and become wastelands.

Venus is an example of what can happen when there is a runaway greenhouse effect. Perhaps by learning more about our twin planet, we'll be able to avoid a similar destiny here on Earth.

Weather

All locations on Earth experience changes in weather. Along the equator temperatures do not vary much, but there is a wet season and a dry season. As one moves toward higher latitudes, both north and south, temperatures become more extreme from one season to the next.

Venus is different. Just as the temperature all over the planet does not change throughout the year, there is never any change from wet to dry, for there is no rainfall. Weather forecasting on Venus would be easy, for one day is the same as every other day.

At the surface of the planet, and up to five or six miles, the atmosphere is calm. Winds blow, but they are soft breezes, rarely reaching ten miles an hour. We learned this when Venera probes landed on the planet, and the information was confirmed by two Vega probes, which passed Venus on their way to a meeting with Halley's comet in 1986. The probes released balloons that floated in the upper part of the atmosphere for several hours. Each balloon carried a gondola with instruments to measure the winds and the makeup of the gases in the atmosphere. And each sent out a lander that transmitted information to Earth.

Winds blow all the time in the upper atmosphere on Venus. They blow 225 miles an hour from east to west— the same direction that Venus rotates. What causes them is not entirely clear.

The pressure of the atmosphere at the surface is very high, 90 times greater than it is on Earth. Normal atmospheric pressure here is 14.7 pounds per square inch at sea level. Living things are adapted to that amount of pressure.

On Venus the pressure is over 1,300 pounds per square inch. Probes that have landed on the planet had to be especially strong to withstand the heat and pressure. Even so, most of the probes lasted only about an hour before the heat and pressure destroyed their instruments.

Venus is hot and dry, and it has crushing atmospheric pressure. It never has bright, unclouded sunshine. We believe it to be a place of constant rumbling as well. The solar wind, a stream of particles that is continuously being ejected by the Sun, is strong at Venus. A good many of the electrically charged particles in the wind become trapped in the Venusian atmosphere. They build up to tremendous levels and create spectacular lightning displays as the charges are released. Frequent rumbles of thunder and flashes of lightning are certainly everywhere on our sister planet.

If you are looking for unusual happenings, for puzzles, and for questions to be answered, you'll find plenty of them on Venus. Just how old are the surface features, and what caused them? Are volcanoes active there today? What events occurred during ancient days on Venus; and what has happened within the last hundred million years or so?

Magellan has been a valuable tool for answering some questions. It has revealed much that is new, and it has proven the accuracy of earlier information. But while the probe has given us lots of answers, it has also raised new and even more challenging questions that will keep scientists searching for answers during the next several decades. Perhaps some of the answers will make it possible for us to better understand our own planet—to us the most important of them all.

Appendices

Spacecraft to Venus

Probe	Nation	Year of Arrival	Purpose
Mariner 2	US	1962	Flyby
Venera 4	USSR	1967	Atmosphere
Mariner 5	US	1967	Flyby
Venera 5	USSR	1969	Atmosphere
Venera 6	USSR	1969	Atmosphere
Venera 7	USSR	1970	Lander
Venera 8	USSR	1972	Lander
Mariner 10	US	1974	Flyby
Venera 9	USSR	1975	Orbiter & lander
Venera 10	USSR	1975	Orbiter & lander
Pioneer Venus	US	1978	Orbiter, atmosphere, radar mapper
Pioneer 13	US	1978	Atmosphere
Venera 11	USSR	1978	Flyby & lander
Venera 12	USSR	1978	Flyby & lander
Venera 13	USSR	1982	Lander
Venera 14	USSR	1982	Lander
Venera 15	USSR	1983	Orbiter, radar mapper
Venera 16	USSR	1983	Orbiter, radar mapper
Vega 1	USSR	1985	Lander & balloon
Vega 2	USSR	1985	Lander & balloon
Magellan	US	1990	Radar mapper

Earth and Venus

	Earth	Venus
Mass (Earth = 1)	1	0.815
Diameter (miles at equator)	7,927	7,503
Density (water = 1)	5.52	5.25
Rotation	23 hours, 56 minutes	243 days
Revolution	365.25 days	224.73 days
Orbital velocity		
(miles per second)	18.54	21.72
(miles per hour)	66,774	78,192
Mean distance from the Sun (millions of miles)	92.75	64.92
Average temperature (degrees Fahrenheit)	59°	860°
Tilt of axis to plane of orbit	23°.45	117°.3
Atmosphere (gases accounting for 90% or more)	nitrogen, oxygen	carbon dioxide

Further Reading

Books and Articles

Bazilevskiy, Aleksandr. "The Planet Next Door." *Sky and Telescope*, April 1989.

Beatty, J. Kelly, and Andrew Chaikin, eds. *The New Solar System*, rev. ed. Cambridge: Cambridge University Press, 1990.

Branley, Franklyn M. *The Nine Planets*. New York: Thomas Y. Crowell, 1978.

———. *Uranus: The Seventh Planet*. New York: Thomas Y. Crowell, 1988.

———. *Saturn: The Spectacular Planet*. New York: Thomas Y. Crowell, 1983.

————. *Neptune: Voyager's Final Target*. New York: Harper-
  Collins, 1992.
————. *Mysteries of the Planets*. New York: Dutton, 1988.
Piel, Jonathan, ed. *Exploring Space*. New York: Scientific
  American Books, 1990.
Powell, Cory S. "Trends in Geophysics: Peering Inward." *Sci-
  entific American*, June 1991, pp. 100–111.
Science magazine, entire section of twelve articles on Venus
  and Magellan. April 12, 1991, pp. 242–311.
Wilhelms, Don. "Venus on a Shoestring." *Air and Space*, Feb-
  ruary/March 1990.

Slides and Booklet

Harrington, Sherwood, and Andrew Fraknoi. *Venus Kit.*
Astronomical Society of the Pacific, 390 Ashton Avenue, San
Francisco, CA 94112.

Index

Numbers in *italics* refer to photographs and illustrations.

Magellan space probe, *2*, *4*, 47
   and detail of Venus's surface,
      1, 5, 26
   discoveries of, 45
   equipment on, 3
   launch and journey of, 1
   new questions raised by, 46
   orbit of, 1, 3, *4*
   pictures from, *18, 20, 22, 23,*
      27–35
   radar of, 3
   scanning range of, 3
magma, 21, 22, 25, 26, 32
magnetism, 36, 38
   Earth's, 37–38
   planets with, 37
   planets without, 37–38
   Venus's lack of, 37–39
Mariner space probes, 47
Mars
   formation of, 15
   lack of magnetism, 37
mass
   of Earth, 15, 48
   of Venus, 15, 48
Maxwell, James Clerk, 36
Maxwell Montes, 36
Mercury
   formation of, 15
   magnetism, 37
   orbit around Sun, 9
   phases, 9
   speed of revolutions, 9
meteorites, 19, 26, 28, 29

See also impact craters
Moon (Earth's), 6

names for features on Venus, 34
neon, 16
Neptune, magnetism of, 37
nickel, 15
nitrogen, 15–16, 48

oceans
   on Earth, 18, 42, 43
   on Venus, 19
orbit
   of Earth, 7, 48
   of Mercury, 9
   outer planets, 9
   velocity, 48
   of Venus, 7, *7*, 9, 11, 48
outer planets, 9
oxygen, 15, 16, 48

phases of Mercury, 9
phases of Venus, 6–7, *7*, 8, *8*
   length of a complete cycle,
      8
Phosphorus ("morning star"), 9, 10,
     10
Pioneer Venus space probe, 5, 26,
     47
plate tectonics, 25, 32
Pluto
   distance from Sun, 9
   magnetism, 38
   speed of revolutions, 9